COUNTRY PROFILE: TURKEY

COUNTRY

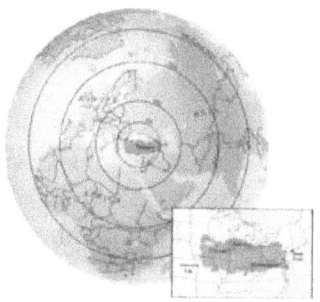

Click to Enlarge Image

Formal Name: Republic of Turkey (Turkiye Cumhuriyeti).

Short Form: Turkey.

Term for Citizen(s): Turk(s).

Capital: Ankara.

Other Major Cities: Istanbul, İzmir (Smyrna), Bursa, Adana, Gaziantep, and Konya (in order of size).

Independence: Turkey celebrates October 29, 1923, the date on which the Republic of Turkey was declared after the fall of the Ottoman Empire, as its date of independence.

Public Holidays: New Year's Day (January 1), National Sovereignty and Children's Day (April 23), Commemoration of Atatürk and Youth and Sports Day (May 19), Victory Day (August 30), the End of Ramadan (September 30–October 2, 2008; variable date determined by the Islamic calendar), Republic Day (October 29), and the Feast of the Sacrifice (December 8–11, 2008; variable date determined by the Islamic calendar).

Flag: The flag has a red background with a white crescent, open to the right, on the left side and a five-pointed white star in the center. The precise origin of the crescent and star symbols, which are quite ancient in the Middle East, is unknown. The flag is an adaptation of the flag of the Ottoman Empire, which preceded the modern Turkish state.

Click to Enlarge Image

HISTORICAL BACKGROUND

The history of the geographic area occupied by the modern state of Turkey and the history of the peoples who occupy that state are quite different. Linking the two is the history of the Ottoman Empire. That empire was a vast, pan-Islamic state that expanded, beginning in the fourteenth century, from a small Turkish emirate located within the boundaries of the present-day Republic of Turkey to include holdings across North Africa, southeastern Europe, and most of the Middle East.

Prehistory and Early History: The land mass occupied by the Asian part of the Republic of Turkey, east of the Sea of Marmara, is known as Anatolia. The region was inhabited by an advanced Neolithic culture as early as the seventh millennium B.C., and metal instruments were in use by 2500 B.C. Late in the third millennium B.C., the warrior Hittites invaded Anatolia and established an empire that made significant economic and administrative advancements. In about 1200 B.C., the Phrygians overthrew the Hittites in western Anatolia, where a Phrygian kingdom then ruled until the seventh century B.C. That kingdom was succeeded by a Lydian kingdom, which in turn was conquered by the Persians in 546 B.C. Meanwhile, beginning in about 1050 B.C., Ionian Greeks began founding cities along the Aegean coast of Anatolia, and in the eighth century B.C., peoples such as the Armenians and the Kurds moved into eastern Anatolia. In the late fourth century B.C., Alexander the Great of Macedonia conquered all of Anatolia. One of the city-states that Alexander founded, Pergamum, became a unique center of wealth and culture. In 133 B.C., Pergamum became the center of a Roman province and remained a cultural center for several centuries. In 330 A.D., the Roman emperor Constantine established the capital of the Greek-speaking half of his empire at Byzantium, on the Sea of Marmara. The city was renamed Constantinople, and the eastern half of the Roman Empire became known as the Byzantine Empire. With its center in Anatolia, the Byzantine Empire remained a powerful entity until the eleventh century. The Patriarchiate of Constantinople, established in the fourth century, represented the Greek-speaking Roman Empire in the Christian church.

Turkish tribes began to migrate westward from China and Central Asia in the seventh century A.D. In 1071 Seljuk Turkish forces defeated a Byzantine army at Manzikert and then occupied all of Anatolia. In the next few centuries, several Seljuk states were established. *Gazi* warriors, tribal horsemen charged with defending the Seljuk frontier, pushed relentlessly westward, and Seljuk governments eventually followed. In 1097 the Christian world responded to this movement with the first in a series of religiously inspired military crusades, which reclaimed part of Anatolia. However, in the next two centuries what was left of the Byzantine Empire fragmented. In the fourteenth century, a new power, the Osmanli Dynasty, came to dominate Anatolia.

The Ottoman Empire: Troops of the Osmanli Dynasty, which gave its name to the Ottoman Empire, moved rapidly into southeastern Europe, defeating Serbian forces at the battle of Kosovo in 1389. Although they were temporarily halted when the Mongol forces of Timur occupied part of Anatolia in the early fifteenth century, in 1453 Ottoman forces captured Constantinople, the last outpost of the Byzantine Empire. The Ottomans renamed Constantinople Istanbul and made it the capital of a new empire and the seat of Sunni Islam as well as Greek Orthodoxy. Under Süleyman the Magnificent (r. 1520–66), the empire expanded across North Africa to Morocco, farther into southeastern Europe, and across the Middle Eastern regions of Kurdistan and Mesopotamia. However, after Süleyman's death the empire began showing signs of decay. The Ottoman navy lost the key Battle of Lepanto to Spanish and Portuguese forces in 1571, and succession struggles shook Istanbul.

Under the leadership of the Köprülü family, the empire made its final push into Europe in the seventeenth century. The siege of Vienna, which was lifted in 1683, marked the farthest extent of Ottoman penetration into Europe. In the years that followed, a multinational European force drove Ottoman troops southward and eastward, forcing the empire to cede substantial territory in Europe in the Treaty of Karlowicz (1699). In the early eighteenth century, Russian Tsar Peter I initiated a long-lasting goal of Russian foreign policy, to gain access to warm-water ports at the expense of the Ottoman Empire. During the next two centuries, Russia fought several wars to diminish Ottoman power. In 1774 the Treaty of Kuchuk-Kaynarja gained Russian ships access to Ottoman waterways. By the nineteenth century, the Ottoman Empire had become known as "the sick man of Europe." The decay of its vast holdings and the nationalist forces that were unleashed in the empire were central issues for all European governments.

In 1832 the European powers forced the Ottoman government to recognize Greek independence after a decade-long Greek guerrilla war. However, Europe also recognized the need to avoid the complete destruction of the empire. In the Crimean War of 1854–56, France and Britain sided with the Ottoman Empire against Russia, which lost the war and ceded some of its power in southeastern Europe. In 1878 the Treaty of Berlin established the independent states of Bulgaria, Romania, and Serbia from former Ottoman territory. In the same period, Britain took possession of Cyprus and Egypt, and France occupied Algeria and Tunisia, further diminishing Ottoman holdings.

Internal conditions also deteriorated in the nineteenth century. Under pressure from the West, between 1839 and 1876 the Ottoman government undertook a series of reforms, collectively known as Tanzimat. Dissatisfaction with reforms stimulated the Young Ottoman movement, which sought Western-style reforms, including secular government and closer relations with Europe. However, in the late 1870s Sultan Abdül Hamid II stifled the reform movement and established a repressive regime. Meanwhile, the empire's financial and geopolitical positions worsened.

In the early 1900s, reformist groups remained active under the repression of Abdül Hamid II. In 1907 the Committee of Union and Progress, better known as the Young Turks, united under military officer Mustafa Kemal, who later took the name Atatürk, "father of the Turks." Between 1909 and 1912, European powers took advantage of a weak Ottoman government to occupy or liberate most of the empire's remaining territory in southeastern Europe. In 1912 the First Balkan War deprived the empire of territory in Macedonia and Thrace. In 1913 these losses led to the overthrow of the government by Enver Pasha, who headed a dictatorial regime of Young Turks during the ensuing war period. The empire regained some European territory during the Second Balkan War of 1913.

When World War I broke out in Europe in 1914, Enver Pasha's alliance with Germany caused Britain, France, and Russia to declare war on the Ottoman Empire. In early 1915, mass deportation of the Armenian population led to the death of as many as 1 million Armenians, an event that remains controversial nearly 100 years later. Atatürk defeated a British amphibious landing at Gallipoli on the Dardanelles later that year. However, in 1916 a successful British campaign cut through the empire's Arab territory, capturing Damascus in 1918. After the empire had suffered numerous defeats, a provisional Ottoman government sued for peace with the Allies.

The Republic of Turkey: After World War I, the provisional government retained control over very little of the former empire. Atatürk led strong nationalist forces seeking to retain Anatolia. In 1921 the nationalists elected Atatürk president of a new government, the Grand National Assembly. In 1922 Atatürk's army repulsed an invading Greek force seeking to expand Greece's postwar allotment of Ottoman territory. The 1923 Treaty of Lausanne, negotiated between the Atatürk government and the Allies, defined control of the Bosporus and the territorial extent of the new Republic of Turkey.

Atatürk's reform program, which became known as Kemalism, aimed at establishing a secular, Europe-oriented state. European name forms and dress styles were encouraged, and the Latin alphabet was adopted. All links between Islam and the state were cut. In 1924 a new constitution guaranteed basic civil rights and prescribed a parliamentary form of government in which the Grand National Assembly would elect the president. Only one party, Atatürk's Republican People's Party, existed, giving the president control of all phases of government. In the 1920s and 1930s, Turkey cautiously sought relations with as many countries as possible. In 1936 Atatürk was able to negotiate a resumption of Turkish control of the Dardanelles and the Bosporus.

World War II found Turkey still in a weakened state. Despite German pressure, the government of Atatürk's successor, Ismet Inönü, maintained neutrality throughout the conflict. In early 1945, Turkey declared war on Germany to ensure it status as one of the charter members of the United Nations. During the Cold War era that followed World War II, Turkey's foreign policy was pro-Western. The Truman Doctrine, which guaranteed the security of postwar Turkey and Greece, resulted in large-scale U.S. military and economic aid to Turkey. However, Turkey's membership in the North Atlantic Treaty Organization (NATO), which it joined in 1952, was complicated by disputes with fellow member Greece over Cyprus and other regional issues. In the 1960s, Turkey and Greece nearly went to war twice over their conflicting views on Cyprus, and in 1974 armed conflict resulted in the partition of the island. Turkey joined a number of other Western alliances and organizations in the 1950s and the 1960s.

In the liberalized postwar atmosphere, party politics became a source of instability and democracy in Turkey. During the 1950s, tensions among the main parties increased as the Democrat Party government of Prime Minister Adnan Menderes became more authoritarian, and the economy suffered inflation and heavy debt. In 1960 Menderes responded to protests by declaring martial law and suspending all political activity. The army, which considered itself the guardian of Atatürk's principles, then replaced Menderes with an interim military government. In the four years following the legislative elections of 1961, the government was an unstable coalition. When the Justice Party, successor to the Democrat Party, gained a majority of seats in the elections of 1965, Süleyman Demirel formed a one-party government. In the late 1960s, the far-right Republican Peasants' Nation Party (later the Nationalist Action Party) began instigating political violence stimulated by economic conditions and resentment of Turkey's pro-Western foreign policy. As the strongest parties continued to lack a parliamentary majority, Turkey suffered a series of weak coalition governments throughout the 1970s, and religious sectarianism gained political influence.

After political and sectarian violence shook Turkey in 1978–79, the Turkish military took power in 1980 to prevent further deterioration. Economic conditions improved significantly in the early 1980s. Civil order was restored at the expense of measures that curtailed human rights. In response to international pressure, a new constitution was ratified in 1982. In the 1980s, the government of General Kenan Evren, leader of the 1980 coup, provided stability as power continued to shift among political parties and coalitions. Evren's former minister of state, Turgut Özal, succeeded him in 1989. The pattern of coalition governments continued in the 1990s. When she became Turkey's first female prime minister in 1993, Tansu Çiller initiated an ambitious privatization program that achieved mixed success. Meanwhile, in the mid-1990s the Kurdistan Workers' Party (PKK) escalated terrorist attacks aimed at gaining Kurdish autonomy in southeastern Turkey, and the Çiller government dropped plans to expand the rights of Turkey's Kurdish minority.

In 1996 a premiership shared between Çiller and Mesut Yılmaz of the conservative Motherland Party failed quickly. When the Yılmaz government resigned, a new coalition government, including the Islamic fundamentalist Welfare Party, took power under Necmettin Erbakan. Alarmed by the increasing social and political power of Islamic institutions, the military forced the resignation of the Erbakan government in 1997. Social tension rose as new regulations secularized public dress and education, and several political leaders were accused of corruption. In 1998 the Welfare Party was dissolved by order of the Constitutional Court for undermining the secular government.

In the late 1990s, Turkey saw progress on several outstanding foreign and domestic issues. Relations with Greece began a long-term process of improvement. Tensions with Greece had remained high throughout the 1980s and 1990s, stimulated by issues such as oil-drilling rights and airspace in the Aegean Sea. In 1996 a dispute over islets in the Aegean, the so-called Imia-Kardak crisis, nearly led to armed conflict between Greece and Turkey. The capture of PKK leader Abdullah Öcalan in 1999 and the group's unilateral cessation of terrorist activity (which lasted until 2004) were major steps forward in Turkey's efforts to subdue Kurdish insurgents in southeastern Turkey. Turkey also moved closer to its long-time goal of full membership in the European Union (EU), which officially approved Turkey's candidacy in 1999.

Following the elections of 1999, Bülent Ecevit formed a new coalition government, which by 2000 had restored some stability. In 1999 and 2000, a series of trials were brought against members of the Welfare Party and other Islamic activists. The stability and economic reforms of 2000 ended with a severe economic crisis and a series of cabinet changes in 2001. In the 2002 parliamentary elections, the secular Islamist Justice and Development Party, indirect successor to the Welfare Party, won a substantial majority of seats in a major shift of parliamentary power. Party leader Tayyip Erdoğan, who became prime minister in 2003, was able to bring his Islamic party into the mainstream of political, economic, and social reform, thus quieting the bitter disputes between advocates of Kemalist secular policy and advocates of an Islamic state. Local elections in 2004 confirmed Erdoğan's popularity. However, the PKK's renunciation in June 2004 of its five-year cease-fire subjected Turkey to numerous terrorist attacks during the following years.

In October 2005, Turkey and the EU began accession negotiations for Turkey's EU membership, a goal supported by traditional enemy Greece. Talks were expected to last 10 years or more because the EU required a wide variety of reforms in Turkey. At the end of 2006, the EU suspended talks on eight of the 35 membership chapters because of Turkey's refusal to recognize formally the Republic of Cyprus, which had joined the EU in 2004. Turkey continued to be the only country recognizing the Turkish Republic of Northern Cyprus, the island's Turkish northern territory, as a legitimate government. The EU was to monitor the entry of Cypriot ships into Turkish ports, a key component of the recognition issue, through 2009. As of mid-2008, no progress had been made in bridging the formidable differences between Greece and Turkey over Cyprus.

In 2007 PKK terrorist attacks in Turkey continued to escalate. In early 2008, Turkey took the controversial step of sending troops over the Iraq border to attack PKK outposts in Iraq's Kurdish north, following a series of bombing raids. PKK activity was diminished by the incursions and by Turkey's enhanced antiterrorist cooperation with the United States, which followed U.S. designation of the PKK as a terrorist organization in 2007.

The question of secular government re-emerged in mid-2007, when the Constitutional Court blocked Prime Minister Erdoğan's selection of Minister of Foreign Affairs Abdullah Gül as a presidential candidate because Gül was not sufficiently secular. Erdoğan himself had been dissuaded from seeking the presidency by large-scale demonstrations by secular factions in Ankara. After Erdoğan's party won parliamentary elections called by the prime minister, Gül's nomination was revived, and parliament approved him as president in August 2007. In October 2007, the near-failure of the presidential nomination process led to approval by national referendum of direct presidential elections.

The role of religion in society remained controversial, however. In February 2008, parliament approved constitutional amendments revoking the ban on women wearing headscarves, a key issue between Islamists and secularists. As a result, the prosecutor general, backed by secular factions, brought an indictment in the Constitutional Court, demanding a shutdown of the ruling Justice and Development Party (AKP) for alleged imposition of sharia (Islamic law). The Constitutional Court annulled the headscarf amendments in June 2008. In July 2008, that court ruled that the AKP need not disband but would lose one-half of its state funding. This compromise ruling left the dispute between Islamists and secularists unresolved.

Another unresolved issue, the historical labeling of the mass deaths of Armenians in Turkey during the early stages of World War I in 1915, remained prominent. In January 2007, a Turkish nationalist extremist assassinated Turkish-Armenian journalist Hrant Dink, who had been outspoken on that issue. The question recurred in late 2007 with the introduction and defeat in the U.S. House of Representatives of Resolution 106, which condemned the deaths as genocide at the hands of the Turks. In Turkey, Article 301 of the penal code, passed in 2005, had made "insulting Turkishness" a crime. The writings of Dink and writer Orhan Pamuk on the genocide issue caused those individuals to be prosecuted under the "Turkishness" statute, whose provisions were weakened in 2008.

GEOGRAPHY

Location: Thrace, the westernmost, European segment of Turkey, forms the southeasternmost extremity of Europe, east of Bulgaria and Greece. Some 8 percent of Turkey's territory is in Thrace.

Click to Enlarge Image

Anatolia, which comprises the bulk of Turkish territory, is a peninsula in western Asia situated between the Black Sea to the north and the Mediterranean Sea to the south. Thrace and Anatolia are separated by the Sea of Marmara and the strategic Dardanelles and Bosporus straits.

Size: The total area of Turkey is 780,580 square kilometers, including 9,820 square kilometers of water.

Land Boundaries: The land boundaries of Turkey are as follows: with Syria, 822 kilometers; Iran, 499 kilometers; Iraq, 352 kilometers; Armenia, 268 kilometers; Georgia, 252 kilometers; Bulgaria, 240 kilometers; Greece, 206 kilometers; and Azerbaijan, 9 kilometers.

Disputed Territory: Turkey has ongoing airspace disputes with Greece in the Aegean Sea region that lies between the two countries, and the division of Cyprus remains an unresolved issue. Syria and Iraq have protested Turkey's confiscation of the headwaters of the Euphrates River, which flows from Turkey into those two countries. Turkey closed its border with Armenia in 1993 in support of Azerbaijan in the Nagorno-Karabakh conflict; the border has remained closed since that time although sporadic talks have occurred.

Length of Coastline: Turkey has 7,200 kilometers of coastline on the Mediterranean Sea, Aegean Sea, Black Sea, and Sea of Marmara.

Maritime Claims: Turkey claims coastline sovereignty extending six nautical miles in the Aegean Sea and 12 nautical miles in the Black and Mediterranean seas. Turkey has a complex set of maritime disputes with Greece in the Aegean Sea.

Topography: Turkey's extremities are divided into the Black Sea coastline region, the Aegean coastline region, the Mediterranean coastline region, and the Arabian Platform along the Syrian border in the south. The interior is divided into the Pontus mountain range, which lines most of the Black Sea coastline; the Taurus mountain range, which extends from the Mediterranean coast north of Cyprus to east-central Anatolia; the Anatolian Plateau, which dominates the interior of western Anatolia; and the eastern highlands, which dominate far eastern Anatolia, east of the Pontus and Taurus chains.

The Black Sea region features rocky coastlines cut by rivers flowing from gorges in the Pontus Mountains. The European and Asian parts of the Aegean region are mainly rolling terrain favorable for agriculture. The narrow Mediterranean coastal region is flat farmland, separated from Anatolia by the Taurus Mountains and opening into wide plains at some points. The Arabian Platform is a region of rolling hills along the Syrian border.

The Pontus or North Anatolian Mountains are lower in the west but rise to more than 3,000 meters in their eastern reaches. The Taurus Mountains are more rugged than the Pontus, but they have fewer rivers and thus form a more complete barrier between the sea and the interior. The Anatolian Plateau extends from the Aegean coastal region between the two major mountain ranges to form the semiarid heartland of Turkey. Elevation is between 600 and 1,200 meters, with several major basins. The eastern highlands are formed by the convergence of the Taurus and Pontus ranges. Mountains here are more rugged than elsewhere in Turkey; the highest mountain, Mt. Ararat, is 5,166 meters high. Turkey's largest lake, Lake Van, is in the eastern highlands.

Principal Rivers: Turkey's longest rivers, the Kızılırmak, Sakarya, and Yeşilırmak, flow northward from the interior of the country into the Black Sea. The Dicle (Tigris) and Firat (Euphrates) originate in the eastern mountains and flow southward across the Arabian Platform into Syria and Iraq. The Büyük Menderes and Gediz are the major rivers flowing from the Anatolian Plateau westward into the Aegean Sea. The Meric (known in Greece as the Evros and in Bulgaria as the Maritsa) forms the border between Greece and Turkish Thrace before flowing into the northern Aegean. The Seyhan flows south from the eastern highlands into the Mediterranean Sea.

Climate: The Aegean and Mediterranean coastal regions have cool, rainy winters and hot, moderately dry summers, with annual precipitation ranging from 580 to 1,300 millimeters. The Black Sea coastal region, whose temperature range is lower than the other coastal regions, has the heaviest rainfall in Turkey, averaging 1,400 millimeters per year. Because it is blocked from the sea by Turkey's mountain ranges, the Anatolian Plateau has a severely continental climate, with extreme cold in the winter (reaching –40° C) and extreme heat in summer. Rainfall there is very sparse in summer, but snowfall in winter is heavy. Annual precipitation averages 400 millimeters. The eastern highlands have hot, dry summers and very cold winters with heavy snowfall.

Natural Resources: Turkey has abundant arable land; its water resources are greater than those elsewhere in the Middle East but generally less than those in European countries. Rivers offer hydroelectric power generation and irrigation. Known oil and natural gas deposits are small, but relatively large amounts of coal are present. Other significant mineral resources are boron and chromium. Long coastlines with a temperate climate support commerce, tourism, and fishing.

Land Use: Some 30 percent of Turkey's land is rated as arable, and another 11.5 percent is used as pasture. About 11 percent of the arable land (3.3 percent of the total) is planted to permanent crops, and 18 percent of the arable land is irrigated.

Environmental Factors: Turkey's main environmental problems are water pollution from the dumping of chemicals and detergents; air pollution, particularly in urban areas; deforestation; and the potential for spills from the 5,000 oil- and gas-carrying ships that pass through the Bosporus annually. The most pressing needs are for water and wastewater treatment plants, solid waste management, and the conservation of biodiversity. The release of pollutants by neighboring countries has critically contaminated the Black Sea, and multinational cooperation has not adequately addressed the problem. Air pollution has accelerated since rapid economic growth began in the mid-1990s. The problem is especially acute in Istanbul, Ankara, Erzurum, and Bursa, where the combustion of heating fuels increases particulate density in winter. Especially in Istanbul, increased car ownership and the slow development of public transportation cause frequent urban smog conditions. Industrial air pollution comes mainly from power plants and the metallurgy, cement, sugar, and fertilizer industries, a large percentage of which lack filtration equipment. Land degradation is a critical agricultural problem, caused by inappropriate use of agricultural land, overgrazing, over-fertilization, and deforestation. Serious soil erosion has occurred in more than half of Turkey's land surface. According to one estimate, Turkey loses 1 billion tons of topsoil annually. Large areas of Turkey are prone to major earthquakes.

The establishment of the Ministry of Environment in 1991 accelerated progress on some environmental problems such as urban air pollution. In the early 2000s, prospective membership in the European Union spurred the updating of some environmental legislation. However, in 2003 the merger of the Ministry of Environment with the Ministry of Forestry reduced the influence of environmental officials in policy making, and enforcement procedures (such as those regulating traffic through the Bosporus) are considered weak. In general, private firms have responded more fully to environmental regulation than state-owned enterprises, which still constitute a large percentage of Turkey's economy.

Time Zone: Turkey's time zone is two hours ahead of Greenwich Mean Time.

SOCIETY

Population: In 2008 the estimated population was 71,893,000. The growth rate, which has decreased sharply in recent decades, was slightly more than 1 percent per year. In 2006 some 68 percent of the population was classified as urban (compared with 27 percent in 1960), and the process of urbanization is expected to continue for the foreseeable future. In 2008 overall population density was 91.9 people per square kilometer. About 25 percent of the population is concentrated around the Sea of Marmara. The fastest rate of growth is in the southeast, which in 2003 accounted for about 10 percent of the total population. In 2008 immigration and emigration rates were equal.

Demography: In 2008 some 24 percent of the population was 14 years of age or younger, and 7 percent was 65 or older. The birthrate, which has declined significantly in recent decades, was 16.2 births per 1,000 population. The fertility rate was 1.87 children per woman. The death rate was 6.02 deaths per 1,000 population, and the infant mortality rate was 37 deaths per 1,000 live births. Life expectancy, which has increased rapidly since 1960, was 70.7 years for males and 75.7 years for females.

Ethnic Groups: Approximately 80 percent of the population is Turkish, and an estimated 17 percent, concentrated in the southeast, is Kurdish. Smaller minority groups include Arabs, Armenians, Greeks, Jews, and Dönme (a small, separate group of Muslims, concentrated in Edirne and Istanbul, whose forbears converted from Judaism). In recent decades, the Armenian, Greek, and Jewish populations have declined steadily. Because of their numbers and their geographic concentration, the Kurds have been by far the most significant ethnic minority. Key issues are the Kurds' demand for autonomy and complaints that they are forbidden to learn Kurdish and forced to abandon their customs.

Languages: The official language is Turkish, which descends from the Old Anatolian Turkish language introduced by the Seljuk Turks who arrived in the eleventh century. Through the centuries, the language has added many loanwords from other languages of the region. Kurdish,

Bulgarian, Armenian, Balkan Gagauz Turkish, Domari, Ladino, and Romany also are used by significant numbers of people. The Latin alphabet has been in use since it superseded the Arabic alphabet in 1928.

Religion: More than 99 percent of the population is Muslim, mostly Sunni. Christianity (Greek Orthodox and Armenian Apostolic) and Judaism are the other religions in practice, but the non-Muslim population declined in the early 2000s. Beginning in the 1980s, the role of religion in the state has been a divisive issue, as influential factions challenged the complete secularization called for by Kemalism and the observance of Islamic practices experienced a substantial revival. In the early 2000s, Islamic groups challenged the concept of the secular state with increasing vigor after the Erdoğan government had calmed the issue in 2003. The Alevi community, a group of non-orthodox Muslims that make up 10–25 percent of the population, has suffered discrimination and occasional massacres. In 2008 the Directorate of Religious Affairs (the government agency that oversees all religious activities in Turkey) proposed establishment of an international faculty of theology, to promote understanding among religions and cultures in Turkey and to improve the understanding of Islam overseas.

Education and Literacy: In 2004 Turkey's overall literacy rate was 87.4 percent, but the rate was only 79.6 percent for females. Eight years of primary education are mandatory between the ages of six and 14, and in the early 2000s the enrollment of male students of those ages was nearly 100 percent. Female enrollment was substantially lower in some rural areas. Three or more years of secondary education are available in general, open, and vocational high schools. In 2008 the United Nations Educational, Scientific and Cultural Organization estimated the attendance rate in secondary school at only 57 percent (48 percent for girls). Islamic Imam Hatip secondary schools expanded rapidly and achieved elite status in the 1990s, but their popularity dwindled in the early 2000s after the government restricted the advanced studies of graduates to religious subjects. Inadequacies of the public system increasingly motivate middle-class parents to seek private education for their children. Because the public program needed wholesale curriculum updates and suffered from over-reliance on rote memorization and standardized examinations, in 2003 Turkey began a comprehensive modernization program in its basic levels (ages six to 14). Teachers have been poorly trained and paid, classes large, and educational quality, geographically uneven. Rural schools generally are poorly equipped. In 2004 the state budget allocated US$6.7 billion, about 6 percent of total expenditures, for education.

In 2006 some 77 universities were in operation, employing 82,000 staff members. Total higher-education enrollment was 2.1 million, including 700,000 at Anadolu University, the only non-residential university. Private universities, which have expanded significantly since 1990, accounted for 4.3 percent of higher-education enrollment. The largest private university is Yeditepe University in Istanbul. Except for the Open University, entrance is by national examination, which made admittance highly competitive in the early 2000s. Turkish university graduates generally are successful in entering international postgraduate programs.

Health: Health care in Turkey is dominated by a centralized state system run by the Ministry of Health (MOH). In 2003 the governing Justice and Development Party introduced a sweeping health reform program aimed at increasing the ratio of private to state health provision and making health care available to a larger share of the population. In the early 2000s, hospital administration has been concentrated more heavily under the MOH, with the goal of giving individual hospitals greater autonomy. At 7.6 percent of gross domestic product in 2005, Turkey's public expenditure on national health was below average for a developed country, although the percentage has increased steadily since 2000. In the early 2000s, about 63 percent of health expenditures came from public sources. In 2006 there was one doctor for every 700 people, one nurse for every 580 people, and one hospital bed for every 380 people. Those ratios are the lowest among European countries. Slightly more than 50 percent of doctors were specialists. The rural population is poorly served by the health-care system, which is much more developed in the western half of the country. Between 80 and 90 percent of the Turks, including self-employed workers, have health care provided by the national pension system, but the low quality of care encourages the use of private health providers in urban areas. Workers in Turkey's large informal economic sector generally lack health coverage. Although the private health industry has grown rapidly since the 1990s, only about 2 percent of the population, mainly in urban areas, has private health insurance. In 2005 about 75 percent of private health expenditures were out-of-pocket rather than being covered by insurance.

The most prevalent causes of death, in order of frequency, are infectious and parasitic diseases, cancer, heart disease, and cerebrovascular diseases. Since the 1980s, the incidence of measles, pertussis, typhoid fever, and diphtheria has decreased sharply because of improved availability of potable water. Malaria and tuberculosis also have decreased noticeably. In 2006 about 90 percent of one-year-olds received inoculations against childhood diseases. Between 1980 and 2004, the infant mortality rate decreased by 65 percent. In 2007 an estimated 3,700 adults in Turkey were infected by the human immunodeficiency virus (HIV). Reportedly, in the early 2000s sexual activity was the cause of 80 to 90 percent of HIV cases, and drug abuse was the cause of 7 percent of cases. Some 260 new cases were reported in 2006. Commercial blood donation has been abolished in order to eliminate that cause of HIV transmission.

Welfare: The state welfare and pension system provides health, welfare, and pension payments to a large majority of citizens. The Social Insurance Law prescribes maternity, illness, on-the-job injury, retirement, and death insurance for all workers except those in agriculture and those who are self-employed. Self-employed workers, including those in agriculture, receive similar coverage under the Social Security Organization for the Self-Employed. In 2000 compulsory unemployment insurance was added to the coverage of the existing law. In the early 2000s, reforms were introduced to make Turkey's system comply more fully with European Union standards. In 2002 a voluntary private pension system was established as a supplement to the mandatory state system. Contributions in the private system are invested in personal retirement accounts, making pension payments dependent on account performance. In 2007 an estimated 26 percent of Turkey's population lived below the poverty level, which was about US$125 per month for a single individual. However, the poverty rate was disproportionately high in the population of the rural east.

ECONOMY

Overview: Nonagricultural economic activity is concentrated in four regions, centered, respectively, around the Sea of Marmara, Edirne on the west coast, the Adana–Mersin–

İskenderun triangle along the Mediterranean Sea, and Ankara. In 2007 a large share of Turkey's major enterprises remained in state hands, including all of the transportation, utilities, and communications infrastructure, many basic industries, and about 30 percent of the assets in the banking sector. After failing to fulfill earlier privatization plans, in 2004 Turkey announced plans to privatize a wide range of industries, including tobacco and sugar processing, communications, and energy. Although no target dates were set, pressure from international financial institutions caused Turkey to begin privatization in most sectors by 2007. Beginning in the 1980s, a number of cities in the Asian part of Turkey, known as the Anatolian Tigers, have shown particular economic growth in the private sector. The economy has been plagued by high inflation and high fiscal deficits. Those conditions improved somewhat beginning in 2004 as private investment increased significantly and the inflation rate declined. The International Monetary Fund has exerted strong pressure and support for reform of the economic system.

Gross Domestic Product (GDP): In 2007 Turkey's estimated GDP of US$663.4 billion (at the official exchange rate) showed a real increase of 5 percent over the previous year. The World Bank forecast an increase of 5.8 percent in 2008. Between 2002 and 2007, the growth rate has been consistently between 5 and 6 percent. The sectoral contribution to GDP was as follows: services 62.8 percent, industry and construction 28.3 percent, and agriculture 8.9 percent. In the early 2000s, the share of agriculture has decreased, the share of industry and construction has remained approximately constant, and the share of services has increased.

Government Budget: In 2006 Turkey's state revenues totaled US$171.3 billion, and its expenditures totaled US$129.4 billion, creating a surplus of US$41.9 billion. In 2005 revenues were US$138 billion and expenditures, US$146.1 billion, resulting in a deficit of US$8.1 billion. In 2004 the deficit was US$30.3 billion. With assistance from International Monetary Fund programs, tax collection has become more efficient in the early 2000s, improving budget administration.

Inflation: Inflation has been a chronic problem in Turkey's economy. Between 1994 and 1999, the average yearly rate was 85 percent. However, in 2004 the rate dropped below 9 percent, the lowest since 1982, and it has remained at about that level since that time. The rate for 2007 was 8.5 percent.

Agriculture: Turkey is self-sufficient in most foods, although some agricultural commodities are imported. A relatively large percentage of Turkey's land is devoted to agriculture, but the productivity of agricultural lands varies greatly. The fields in western Turkey and along the southern coast are most productive, but physical conditions and greater transportation distances make agriculture substantially less profitable in other regions. The principal agricultural exports are cotton, fruits, hazelnuts, tobacco, and wheat. Other important agricultural products are barley, corn, oilseeds, olives, potatoes, sugar beets, and tea. The most important livestock are cattle, chickens, goats, and sheep, but livestock raising has declined significantly since the 1980s. The efficiency of the agricultural sector is limited by the predominance of small, non-mechanized farms on which a disproportionately large segment of the population (27 percent in 2007) depends for its livelihood. Output varies substantially according to weather conditions. The Southeastern Anatolia Project, a federal program aimed at raising the development level of nine of Turkey's most impoverished provinces, has a substantial agricultural component. Among the project's goals is an extensive series of dams and canals in the Firat (Euphrates) Valley, scheduled for completion in 2010. The project will provide irrigation to improve agricultural productivity in the southeast. State support, an important component of agricultural enterprises, often has been poorly distributed and without proportionate returns. In the early 2000s, the government reduced agricultural support and began restructuring marketing systems.

Forestry: In 2000 the extent of Turkey's forests was estimated at 10.2 million hectares. However, the forests of eastern Anatolia are not suitable for harvesting. The only usable timber comes from the Black Sea coastal region, and timber does not make a significant contribution to the economy. Because poor management and infrequent cutting have left many forests over-mature, only about 20 percent of the total forested area is classified as commercially exploitable. In 2003 Turkey's timber industry produced a total of 16 million cubic meters of wood products, about 32 percent of which was fuelwood. Forest protection by the state is handicapped by the dependence of local populations on trees for fuel. In 2004 forestry contributed 0.4 percent of gross domestic product.

Fishing: Despite Turkey's long coastline, fishing is not an important contributor to the economy. The fishing industry is concentrated on the coasts of the Black Sea and the Sea of Marmara, where output has been cut by pollution and over-fishing. In 2002 Turkey's fish catch totaled 567,000 tons, a substantial decrease from the annual totals of the 1990s. Anchovies accounted for more than 60 percent of the catch. A small aquaculture industry also exists. In 2004 fishing contributed 0.4 percent of gross domestic product.

Mining and Minerals: Turkey's major mining operations, formerly controlled by state-owned companies, were increasingly privatized in the early 2000s. During that period, aluminum, chrome, copper, and silver mines moved into the private sector. Boron, of which Turkey has 60 percent of the world supply, is the most important non-fuel mineral. Its extraction remains a state monopoly. Based on new discoveries and foreign investment in the early 2000s, the output of gold and soda ash have increased significantly. Gold reserves are estimated at 450 tons. By far the most important mineral product is lignite coal, reserves of which were estimated at 10.6 billion tons in 2008. Turkey's low-quality lignite, burned mainly in power stations, is highly polluting. The output of hard coal has declined, reaching 3.3 million tons in 2002. Hard coal reserves are estimated at 1.2 billion tons. Marble is the most important mineral export.

Industry and Manufacturing: Turkey's diverse manufacturing sector satisfies domestic demand for a wide variety of products; the main manufactured exports are consumer goods. Textiles and clothing account for 15 percent of all manufacturing and about one-third of manufactured exports. However, much of this production is unreported because it is in the "informal" sector. The most important textile product is cotton cloth. Besides textiles, the most important consumer items produced are televisions, automobiles, refrigerators, washing machines, and vacuum cleaners. The most important heavy industrial products are processed fuels, steel, cement, tractors, and fertilizers. Most manufacturing enterprises are privately owned, but the size of such enterprises varies greatly, and the state has influenced the relative growth of industries by providing disproportionate investment and incentives. Multinational companies are present in many light and heavy industries. Foreign auto companies—Fiat, Honda, Hyundai, Renault, and Toyota—have plants in Turkey. The industry produced nearly 1 million vehicles in

2006. Other industries such as appliances are mainly Turkish-owned. A large proportion of the appliances, consumer electronics, and vehicles manufactured in Turkey are exported. The largest privately owned industrial company is the Arcelik firm, which manufactures a wide variety of consumer products.

Traditionally, the construction industry has made an important contribution to the economy. However, construction's contribution declined in the late 1990s and early 2000s because of a reduction in demand for domestic and foreign building projects and because of Turkey's 2001 economic crisis. Expansion resumed at a moderate rate in 2004, and in 2005 and 2006 the growth rate was about 20 percent per year. In the early 2000s, the industry's foreign operations expanded, particularly in Russia, Turkmenistan, Kazakhstan, Saudi Arabia, and Afghanistan.

Energy: Coal is the only fossil fuel that Turkey possesses in abundance, meaning that large amounts of oil and natural gas are imported. In the early 2000s, the domestic distribution of fuels and electricity has been reformed to meet European Union standards. Distribution of natural gas, nearly all of which is imported, is to be privatized by 2009. Since the 1990s, Turkey has attempted to substitute cleaner natural gas for highly polluting domestic coal. In the early 2000s, about two-thirds of the 1.1 billion cubic feet of natural gas that Turkey imported was used by the electric power industry. Russia is the main supplier of natural gas; its share of Turkey's total imports is expected to rise from the 2003 figure of 25 percent to 58 percent in 2010. Other major suppliers are Iran and Azerbaijan. In 2005 Turkey's domestic oil output was about 45,000 barrels per day, about half the level of 1990, and it was forecast to fall by nearly 50 percent by 2011. Turkey imports about 90 percent of its oil, mainly from Iran, Iraq, Russia, Saudi Arabia, and Syria. The demand for oil is expected to grow by about 20 percent from 2006 to 2011. Turkey's location along several international oil and gas pipelines eases transport. Ceyhan, on the Black Sea coast, is the terminus of the Baku–Tbilisi–Ceyhan oil pipeline, which was completed in 2006.

Because the demand for electric power doubled in the 1990s, Turkey became a net importer of electricity, as domestic generating capacity was unable to keep up with demand. Although in 2006 Turkey's generating capacity of 35,000 megawatts exceeded demand, plans called for increasing that amount to 67,000 megawatts by 2010 in anticipation of increased demand. In the early 2000s, domestic power supply was inefficient because new plants came online slowly, and industry privatization stalled. Occasional power outages have occurred, and electricity costs are among the highest in Europe. In 2008 a deal with Iran linked the two countries' electric systems, providing Turkey a backup supply when its grid fails. In 2007 TEAS, the state power generation and distribution company, still controlled 90 percent of the electric power market through its 15 thermoelectric and 30 hydroelectric plants. However, most of the plants in the next expansion phase are to be privately owned. Since 2002 an independent Energy Market Regulatory Authority has overseen privatization and distribution. This agency is considered an important improvement in Turkey's energy management. Turkey abandoned plans for its first nuclear power plant in 2000 and again in 2005; in 2007 a controversial new plan called for a nuclear plant to open at Sinop in 2014. Turkey is considered to have substantial unused supplies of hydroelectric, wind, and solar power.

Services: In the early 2000s, the contribution of service industries to the gross domestic product has increased (from 53 percent in 1998 to more than 60 percent in 2007), particularly in the areas of trade, catering, and personal services. Banking, the most important of Turkey's financial services, has undergone significant changes in the early 2000s. The current system is based on the Banks Act of 2005, which improved the inspection system, raised the standards for institutional participation in the industry, and simplified the process of bank mergers and takeovers. The financial crisis of 2001, for which the banks were partly responsible, had a severe impact on the sector. The resulting rationalization of the banking system reduced the number of banks by about one-third to 36, leaving the five largest banks with more than 50 percent of total assets. Those five private banks are part of large conglomerates with interests in many other sectors. Three state banks control about 30 percent of the industry's assets; their privatization has proceeded slowly. Beginning in 2005, the participation of foreign banks had increased substantially.

Since the 1990s, the Istanbul Stock Exchange has been quite active, although political developments have caused substantial volatility. Between 2004 and 2006, daily trading volume increased by 65 percent. In 2004 the exchange listed 291 companies, including some of the largest in Turkey. However, equity in many companies is unavailable for public trading.

Most of Turkey's large insurance companies are connected with banks or international insurance firms. Per capita insurance expenditures, averaging US$80 per year in 2005, are the lowest in the industrialized world. Reform of the industry's regulatory structure, a requirement for membership in the European Union, has been proposed and tabled for several years. Until such reform, the National Treasury is the regulating agency.

Small enterprises have dominated retail trade. However, in the early 2000s large Turkish chains such as Migros, Gima, and Tansas and foreign companies such as Metro of Germany, Carrefour of France, and Tesco of Britain occupied an expanding share of the retail sector. Shopping malls and supermarkets are increasingly common.

Turkey has taken advantage of its wide variety of scenic and historic locations, particularly along its southern and western coasts, to build a substantial tourism industry based on local ownership of hotels and restaurants. Some 19.8 million tourists visited Turkey in 2006, an increase of 90 percent over 2000. This activity generated revenues estimated at US$16.9 billion and provided an important source of foreign currency.

Labor: In 2007 Turkey's labor force was estimated at 23.5 million. However, a large part of this force (officially estimated at 11 million in 2004) works in the "informal sector," making measurement of its activities difficult. Another 3 million work in European Union and Middle Eastern countries. About 41 percent of the official workforce is occupied in services, 36 percent in agriculture, and 23 percent in construction and industry. In the early 2000s, the shift of labor away from agriculture and into services accounted for a significant increase in overall labor productivity. Industrial labor is heavily unionized, but the government has restricted some union activities. The largest unions are the Turkish Confederation of Labor and the Labor Unions Confederation. Total union membership is estimated at 3 million.

In early 2008, unemployment was estimated at 10.8 percent overall, compared with 10.4 percent in 2007. However, unemployment among the youngest age cohorts was estimated at nearly 20 percent. The overall rate was 12.7 percent in urban areas and 7.6 percent in rural areas. Another 4 percent of the workforce was considered underemployed.

Although inflation has depressed wage values, in the early 2000s a series of sharp increases brought the 2008 minimum wage to US$483 per month. Wage disparities are great between eastern and western Turkey. Women account for only about one-quarter of the overall workforce but for 60 percent of the agricultural workforce. Remittances from Turks working abroad, chiefly in Germany and Saudi Arabia, have been an important source of national income. In the early 2000s, annual remittance figures have varied considerably, in part because of economic cycles in Turkey. The highest figure was US$5 billion in 1998.

Foreign Economic Relations: Beginning in the late 1970s, Turkey has liberalized what was a policy of import substitution and protection of domestic industries by import restrictions. In the 1990s, export subsidies were abolished, and trade with the European Union (EU) increased slowly and steadily. Turkey was admitted to the World Trade Organization (WTO) in 1995. In 1996 a customs union was established between Turkey and the EU, abolishing tariffs on industrial products for both sides. The same relationship was established with all countries entering the EU after 1996, with the exception of Cyprus. An agreement on agricultural products retains tariffs on some agricultural imports from EU countries. In 1999 Turkey revised its customs legislation in accordance with EU standards. Between 1990 and 2007, the EU share of Turkey's exports remained steady between 51 and 56 percent, and the EU share of Turkey's imports also remained steady between 42 and 47 percent. Throughout that period, Germany remained among Turkey's primary trade partners, although that country's percentage of total trade (11.4 percent of exports and 10.6 percent of imports in 2006) diminished steadily in the early 2000s. In the early 2000s, both export and import trade with the United States declined somewhat. In 2007 the United States accounted for 6 percent of Turkey's exports, compared with 7.7 percent in 2004, and for 4.5 percent of its imports, compared with 5 percent in 2004. In the early 2000s, a larger share of Turkey's imports came from the Commonwealth of Independent States (CIS), mainly because of reliance on natural gas from Russia, than had been the case during the 1990s. In 2007 Russia accounted for 12.8 percent of Turkey's imports (overtaking Germany as the largest import supplier), and the CIS as a whole accounted for 8.2 percent of Turkey's exports. Turkey also has bilateral trade relationships with the member nations of the European Free Trade Association (Iceland, Liechtenstein, Norway, and Switzerland), Albania, Bosnia and Herzegovina, Croatia, Egypt, Israel, Macedonia, Morocco, the Palestinian Territories, and Syria.

In the early 2000s, agricultural products dropped below 10 percent of Turkey's exports. Minerals and mineral products accounted for about 5 percent. In 2006 finished textiles accounted for about 23 percent. Other important exported manufactured products were steel, construction materials, appliances, televisions, and motor vehicles. Substantial unofficial trade occurs with neighboring countries of the Middle East and the CIS. The value of such trade in 2006 was estimated at US$6.4 billion. Fuels are the leading "official" imported commodity. Others are chemical products and machinery and transport equipment. Russia and Saudi Arabia are the chief suppliers of fuels. Other major suppliers of imports are the EU countries, Switzerland, Japan, and China. Between 2004 and 2006, imports from China more than doubled.

Trade Balance: In 2007 Turkey's imports had a total value of US$156.9 billion, and its exports were valued at US$110.5 billion. Thus, the trade deficit for 2007 was US$46.4 billion, continuing a persistent trend. Between 2003 and 2006, the trade deficits were, respectively, US$21.8 billion, US$25 billion, US$28.7 billion, and US$35.7 billion.

Balance of Payments: In the early 2000s, Turkey's balance of payments has varied widely, although it was negative every year from 2000 through 2004. In 2007 the current account showed a deficit of US$38 billion, and the capital account showed a surplus of US$48.5 billion. The overall balance of payments for 2007 was US$12 billion.

External Debt: In 2007 Turkey's external debt totaled US$240 billion. When measured as a percentage of gross domestic product, this amount was a decrease of 7 percent compared with the average percentage (57 percent) for the years 2002–6.

Foreign Investment: Because of political uncertainty and the structure of Turkey's investment system, foreign direct investment (FDI) was relatively low in the first years of the 2000s, exceeding US$2 billion in only one year between 1999 and 2004. The total for 2004 was about US$2 billion, but legislative changes stimulated substantial increases beginning in 2005. Between 2005 and 2007, the total increased from US$8.7 billion to US$22 billion. FDI increases in 2006 were based particularly on activity in the banking and telecommunications sectors. In early 2008, foreign portfolio investment was estimated at about US$100 billion. A US$1.5 billion power plant near İskenderun, completed in 2004 by the STEAG utilities company of Germany, is the largest direct investment ever by a German company in Turkey. Automotive companies in France, Italy, Japan, South Korea, and the United States participate in multinational partnerships with Turkey. In 2004 a Japanese consortium began building a railroad tunnel under the Bosporus, scheduled for completion in 2010. The United States–based General Dynamics Corporation has invested substantially in fighter aircraft manufacture in Turkey, and in the early 2000s Turkey's arms procurement policy encouraged joint projects and the licensing of production of foreign designs.

Currency and Exchange Rate: In January 2005, a currency reform established the new Turkish lira, which was worth 1 million of the previous unit, the Turkish lira. In August 2008, the exchange rate was about 1.2 new Turkish liras to the U.S. dollar. Thus, in 2008 the new lira was stronger against the dollar than the old lira had been in 2003, when the average rate was slightly more than 1.5 million to the dollar.

Fiscal Year: Turkey's fiscal year is the calendar year.

TRANSPORTATION AND TELECOMMUNICATIONS

Transportation Overview: The development of efficient domestic transportation systems in Turkey has been slowed by long distances, difficult terrain, and low investment. Major investment projects are expected to improve the national road and railroad systems by 2010.

Roads: Roads are Turkey's most important domestic transportation system, although only 177,000 kilometers of paved roads were in service in 2004. More than 250,000 kilometers of existing roads are unpaved. The state and provincial system includes about 61,000 kilometers of roads, 1,900 kilometers of which are classified as highways. Main highways radiate from Ankara in central Anatolia; Istanbul and İzmir in the west; Adana in the south; and Erzurum and Diyarbakır in the east. The most important recent additions to the system are the Ankara–Istanbul toll road and the Black Sea Coast Road, which was completed in 2007. Because the number of motor vehicles increased eightfold between 1983 and 2007 (when it exceeded 10 million), Turkey's city streets are very congested. Congestion has inspired some cities to revive their tramway systems. In the early 2000s, several major road and bridge projects were under discussion to link Anatolia more effectively with Europe. In 2007 the completion of the Bolu Tunnel between Istanbul and Ankara cleared a major obstacle in the E–5 Highway linking Europe with the Middle East.

Railroads: In 2006 Turkey had only 8,697 kilometers of rail lines, all standard gauge and mostly in service for more than 60 years. Most major population centers are connected by rail. From a ring around the Anatolian Plateau, rail lines radiate to Zonguldak and Samsun on the Black Sea; Istanbul, İzmir, and Bandırma in the west; and via Adana to Syria and Iraq in the south. Three lines go into eastern Anatolia. The state-owned system is slow and unprofitable. In 2006 only 4 percent of freight transport and 2 percent of passenger transport were by rail. Between 1990 and 2003, passenger trips decreased by 50 percent. Planned improvements include limited privatization, upgrading of the Istanbul–Ankara trunk line to include high-speed trains, and improved rail links between Anatolia and Thrace. The Marmaray project, scheduled for completion in 2012, aims to improve rail transportation through Istanbul to Europe. It will include a railroad tunnel under the Bosporus. Ankara, Bursa, Istanbul, and İzmir have limited metro systems; lines in Ankara and İzmir were expanding in the early 2000s, and a line is under construction in Adana.

Ports: Turkey's ports have suffered from overcrowding and inefficiency. The main facilities are located at Antalya, İskenderun, and Mersin on the Mediterranean; Bandırma, Gemlik, Istanbul, and İzmit in the Marmara region; İzmir on the Aegean Sea; and Hopa, Samsun, and Trabzon on the Black Sea. The largest port, İzmir, has an annual capacity of 11 million tons and handles almost 40 percent of Turkey's shipping. The ports of Istanbul, İzmir, İzmit, and Mersin are particularly vital because they are outlets for large industrial regions, and the Marmara ports are vital because of the high volume of foreign freight that passes through them. The Aegean and Marmara ports handle most of Turkey's container ship traffic, which is projected to increase dramatically between 2008 and 2020. The state railroad and the Turkish Maritime Administration have managed all the largest ports. However, many smaller ones were privatized between 1997 and 2003. The operation of Mersin was leased to a private company in 2005, and those of Bandırma and Samsun were similarly converted in 2008. The privatization of İzmir, considered vital to its modernization, has been delayed by lawsuits. In the early 2000s, Turkey's 11-million-ton merchant marine has carried a decreasing share of the total freight passing through its ports; in 2007 less than 20 percent of port traffic was under the Turkish flag. Passenger ships in Istanbul are important commuter carriers.

Inland Waterways: Turkey has about 1,200 kilometers of inland waterways, none of which offers a vital line of transportation. Not included in that amount is the channel formed by the Dardanelles, the Sea of Marmara, and the Bosporus, linking the Black Sea with the Mediterranean Sea and forming one of the most important water connections in the world. In the early 2000s, safety and environmental factors have made expansion of traffic through this heavily traveled route problematic.

Civil Aviation and Airports: Of Turkey's 90 mainly state-owned airports with paved runways operating in 2007, 15 had runways longer than 3,000 meters. Some 18 heliports also were in operation. The three largest airports are located at Istanbul, Ankara, and İzmir. Istanbul-Atatürk, the largest airport, was expanded in 2000, as was the primary tourist airport at Ankara. In 2007 the largest airline, Turk Hava Yollari (THY, Turkish Airlines), flew from Ankara and Istanbul to 104 international destinations, including major cities in Europe and the United States. The airline announced 11 new destinations in 2008. In 2007 THY, which was privatized in 2007 and reorganized in 2008, flew 19.6 million passengers, an increase of 16 percent over 2007 and nearly twice the number flown in 2001. In the first half of 2008, passenger flights increased by 16 percent over the same period of 2007. About 55 percent of passengers were on domestic flights. The activity of rival domestic airlines, such as Atlas Jet, Onur Air, and Pegasus Airlines, increased in the early 2000s, carrying about 2 million passengers in 2004.

Pipelines: In 2007 Turkey had 7,511 kilometers of natural gas pipelines and 3,636 kilometers of oil pipelines. In the early 2000s, controversial pipeline issues were Turkey's role in new routes bringing oil and natural gas from the flourishing Caspian Sea region into Europe and the configuration of a new pipeline that would connect Russia with the Mediterranean and bypass the Bosporus. The potentially lucrative Baku–Tbilisi–Ceyhan (BTC) line, 1,000 kilometers of which passes through Turkey, began bringing oil from the Caspian in 2006. That line is advantageous because it bypasses both Russia and the crowded Bosporus corridor. Because the BTC line's volume of 1 million barrels per day is considered insufficient for the future, Turkey has engaged in international discussions about several other pipeline routes that would bypass the Bosporus. Turkey's status as a European energy hub improved in late 2007 with the opening of a pipeline between Turkey and Greece (one leg of the Turkey–Greece–Italy Pipeline, to be fully operational in 2012), which will supplement Europe's access to oil from the Caspian Sea region.

Telecommunications: In the 1980s and 1990s, Turkey's telecommunications systems underwent substantial modernization, including nearly complete digitization and advanced intercity trunk lines. In 2006 some 19 million main telephone lines and 52.6 million cellular phones were in use. A satellite system links users in remote areas. In 2005 three private mobile services, totaling about 30 million subscribers, were operating. Turk Telekom, the state-owned telecommunications monopoly, was partially privatized in 2005 in a sale to the Oger firm of

Saudi Arabia. As Internet usage has increased dramatically (reaching 16 million in 2007, an increase of 57 percent over 2005), demand has exceeded the supply of Internet and data services.

GOVERNMENT AND POLITICS

Overview: The present constitution was adopted in November 1982 and amended in 1995, 1999, 2001, 2004, and 2007. The government is a parliamentary system in which, until a constitutional amendment in 2007 provided for direct popular election, the president was elected by the legislative branch. Power is highly centralized at the national level. Since the adoption of a multiparty system in 1946, most of Turkey's governments have been coalitions of two or more parties. Many of those governments have been weak and ephemeral. The government chosen in 2002 was the first since 1991 to be formed by a single majority party, the Justice and Development Party (AKP). As of mid-2008, that party retained strong public support, although an indictment in the Constitutional Court for antisecular activity had jeopardized the government of Prime Minister Tayyip Erdoğan. The court ruled in July 2008 that the party need not disband but revoked half the party's state funding. The military has taken power three times, in 1960, 1971, and 1980. Although in each case elections were held within three years, the military remains an important political force. In the 1990s and early 2000s, the power of Islamist parties has increased, despite the principle of strictly secular government established by Mustafa Kemal Atatürk, the first president of modern Turkey. The judicial branch is considered to be genuinely independent.

Executive Branch: Prior to October 2007, the constitution called for election of the president by the Turkish Grand National Assembly (TGNA, parliament) for a single term of seven years. The last presidential election under that provision was in August 2007. However, following that election a national referendum amended the constitution to provide for direct popular election of the president for a five-year term, with eligibility for one additional term. The president, who has limited powers and abdicates party membership upon election, appoints the prime minister and has the power to summon sessions of the TGNA, promulgate laws, and ratify international treaties. The president also is commander of the armed forces. President Ahmet Sezer (in office 2000–2007) came into conflict with successive governments of Tayyip Erdoğan (appointed prime minister in 2003) over a number of issues. The prime minister, who supervises the implementation of government policy, usually is the head of the majority or plurality party of the TGNA. Members of the Council of Ministers, which in 2008 included 24 full ministers and three deputy prime ministers, are nominated by the prime minister and approved by the president. The president also appoints members of the national courts and the heads of the Central Bank and broadcasting organizations, and the president has the power to dissolve the Grand National Assembly. The president presides over the National Security Council, whose members include the prime minister; the chief of the General Staff; the ministers of national defense, interior, and foreign affairs; and the commanders of the branches of the armed forces and the gendarmerie. This powerful body sets national security policy and coordinates all activities related to military mobilization and defense.

Legislative Branch: Legislative power is exercised by the Turkish Grand National Assembly (TGNA), a one-chamber parliament composed of 550 deputies, whose constitutionally mandated five-year terms were reduced to four-year terms by the constitutional amendment of 2007. The TGNA writes legislation, supervises the Council of Ministers, and adopts the budget. Until the amendment of 2007, the TGNA also elected the president, by a two-thirds majority, from among its members. The president can be voted out of office by a vote of three-quarters of TGNA members. The TGNA decides on declaring war, martial law, and emergency rule and approves international agreements. Parliamentary elections are based on proportional representation subject to a national threshold of 10 percent of the vote. Members are elected by lists drawn up by party leaders. Once elected, members have immunity from prosecution. TGNA legislation is developed by specialized commissions. The laws passed by the TGNA are promulgated by the president within 15 days. The president may refer a law back to the assembly for reconsideration.

Judicial Branch: The highest court in Turkey is the Constitutional Court, which examines the constitutionality of laws and other government actions. Members of that court, which in the early 2000s increasingly became a bastion of secularism, are appointed by the president. The Court of Cassation, which is divided into 30 specialized chambers whose members are appointed by a Supreme Council of Judges and Prosecutors (in turn appointed by the president), hears appeals from lower courts. The military court system, whose top level is the Military Court of Appeals, hears only cases related to the military. The Council of State settles administrative cases and offers opinions on laws drafted by the Council of Ministers. A 2004 amendment to the constitution abolished State Security Courts (SSCs), which had been cited for human rights violations as they carried out their function of trying individuals deemed a threat to national interests. However, the Heavy Penal Courts, appointed to replace the SSCs under the new Criminal Procedure Code of 2005, received similar powers, and the term SSC still is in common usage.

Administrative Divisions: Turkey is divided into 81 provinces (*iller*; sing., *il*), which in turn are divided into districts and sub-districts. Provinces have an average of eight districts each. Sixteen large metropolitan municipalities, about 3,200 smaller towns, and about 50,000 villages have their own local governments.

Provincial and Local Government: The provinces are administered by governors, who are appointed by the Council of Ministers with the approval of the president. The governors function as the principal agents of the central government and report to the Ministry of Interior. Districts are administered by sub-governors. Provinces, districts, and local jurisdictions also have directly elected councils. Although local jurisdictions have gained political powers since 1980, the system remains highly centralized. The national government oversees elected local councils in order to ensure the effective provision of local services and to safeguard the public interest; the minister of interior is empowered to remove from office local administrators who are being investigated or prosecuted for offenses related to their duties. Several ministries of the national government have offices at the provincial and district levels. An autonomous local administration exists at the level of municipalities, which elect a mayor and a municipal council. In the villages, the village assembly elects a council of elders and a village headman.

Judicial and Legal System: When the Republic of Turkey was established, the Islamic law of the Ottoman Empire was replaced in 1926 with a secular system borrowed from the Swiss and Italian legal codes. The judicial system has been criticized for the influence of the executive branch, particularly the National Security Council, over adjudication of certain cases. Also criticized is the membership of the minister of justice, a member of the executive branch, on the powerful Supreme Council of Judges and Prosecutors, whose functions of overseeing the lower courts and choosing judges have no review mechanism. Prosecutors have wide authority in the investigation of cases. All cases are heard by judges, not by juries. Minor civil and penal cases are assigned to civil and penal courts of the peace, respectively. Every province also has one penal and at least one civil court of first instance, each consisting of one judge, to hear routine cases assigned to the next level. Central criminal courts, of which Turkey has 172, hear more serious criminal cases. Those courts consist of a judicial panel of three. Commercial courts are a branch of the civilian court system, handling all cases arising from business and trade relationships. Some 35 such courts were in operation in 2007. In 2002 Turkey abolished application of the death penalty in peacetime. A new penal code, responding to some but not all of the membership requirements of the European Union (EU), went into effect in June 2005.

Electoral System: Suffrage is universal for citizens 18 years of age and older. As of the constitutional referendum of October 2007, the president is elected by popular vote to a term of five years, with one additional term possible. This amendment abolished the system by which the Grand National Assembly elected the president, who under that system required two-thirds of assembly votes to be elected in the first or second round of voting. Direct parliamentary and local elections are held (separately) every four years (reduced from five by the 2007 constitutional amendment), but the president or the Grand National Assembly can declare elections at an earlier date. The assembly called the 2007 parliamentary elections four months ahead of the scheduled date because of a crisis over selection of the next president. (That crisis later triggered the constitutional referendum on presidential elections when President Ahmet Sezer vetoed legislation calling for direct election of the president.) As it had in the 2002 parliamentary elections, in 2007 the Justice and Development Party won a majority of seats and formed a one-party government on that basis.

Political Parties: Turkey has had a multiparty system since 1946, but restrictions on the formation of new parties and the potential for the judiciary to disband parties have been controversial issues. Although constitutional amendments in 1995 and 2001 limited the conditions under which the Constitutional Court may disband a party, in 2008 that court was able to consider closing down the ruling Justice and Development Party (AKP) for violating the requirement of secular governance. The existence and alignments of Turkey's political parties have been fleeting, although the Republican People's Party, founded by Atatürk in 1923, still had the second-largest representation in parliament in 2008. After the parliamentary elections of 2002 caused a major shift in party strength, only two parties—the Republican People's Party and the AKP—held seats in parliament. In the elections of 2007, the ultranationalist Nationalist Movement Party won 71 seats, becoming the third party represented in parliament. The AKP held the majority (341 of 550 seats), despite losing 23 seats compared with the previous allocation. As in 2003, its head, Tayyip Erdoğan, was named prime minister following the 2007 elections. Some 26 seats were held nominally by independents, who in fact represented Islamic parties. Party representation in the Grand National Assembly is proportional to total votes received by a party's candidates, but those candidates must receive at least 10 percent of the total vote for the party to be represented. The officially unrepresented parties receiving the most votes in the elections were the center-right Democratic Party (formerly the True Path Party), the nationalist secular Youth Party, and the Islamic fundamentalist Felicity Party.

Mass Media: Turkey has a wide variety of domestic and foreign periodicals expressing diverse views, and domestic newspapers are extremely competitive. The media exert a strong influence on public opinion. Media ownership is concentrated among large private companies, a factor that limits the views that are presented. The largest such operator is the highly diversified Dogan Group, which is the fifth-largest conglomerate in Turkey. Dogan owns two major newspapers and three national television stations. Dogan's newspapers were estimated to occupy about 50 percent of the market in 2008. The most popular daily newspapers are *Hürriyet*, *Milliyet*, *Posta*, *Sabah*, *Yeni Asir*, and *Zaman*. Of those titles, *Zaman* (860,000) and *Posta* (645,000) have the largest circulation. *Milliyet* and the daily *Cumhuriyet* are among the most respected serious newspapers. The most popular English-language newspapers are *Today's Zaman* and *Turkish Daily News*. Most newspapers are based in Istanbul, with simultaneous Ankara and İzmir editions. The broadcast media have very wide dispersion because satellite dishes and cable systems are widely available. Through its parliament-appointed National Broadcasting Council, the government exerts strong control over those media, discouraging discussion of controversial topics. The largest television broadcast outlet is Turkish Radio and Television (TRT, the state-owned outlet), which broadcasts via five national and two international channels. In addition, in 2005 there were 14 national private television stations and 33 national private radio stations. Major private television companies, a category legalized in 1993, include Star TV, Kanal D, Show TV, and NTV. TRT's radio broadcasts go through six national channels. Major private radio outlets include Capital Radio and Show Radio. A major shift toward support of the government occurred in 2008 with the sale of KanalTurk, an intensely antigovernment national television station, to an associate of Prime Minister Erdoğan. Foreign companies may own as much as 25 percent of a Turkish media enterprise. In 2005 some 37.8 million televisions were in service. Aside from Turkish, the state radio network offers some programs in Arabic, Bosnian, Circassian, and Kurdish.

Foreign Relations: In 2008 the center of Turkey's foreign relations remained the United States and Western Europe. Relations with Greece, a long-time antagonist, began to improve in 1999. Talks with Greece on reunification of Cyprus were frozen in 2004, but in 2008 the new regime of Demetris Christofias in the Republic of Cyprus called for resumption. The claims of Greece and Turkey to territorial waters and the continental shelf between them in the Aegean Sea remained in sharp conflict in 2008. Although the two countries' fundamental dispute over Cyprus still was unresolved, Turkey maintained Greece's support for membership in the European Union (EU). However, between 2004 and 2008 domestic support for Turkey's EU membership dropped from 70 percent to 40 percent. Relations with the United States, close since the beginning of the Cold War, were damaged in 2003 when Turkey refused to allow U.S. troops to cross into Iraq from Turkey. The United States canceled a major aid package, which later was restored in a smaller form. The United States continued advocating Turkey's membership in the EU during this period. In 2006 a "shared vision document," identifying strategic bilateral goals, reduced tensions. However, in 2007 the near-passage by the U.S. House of Representatives of an "Armenian Genocide Resolution" threatened to chill relations once again.

In the 1990s, Turkey developed economic relationships with the Turkic republics of the former Soviet Union—Azerbaijan, Kazakhstan, Kyrgyzstan, Turkmenistan, and Uzbekistan—and economic and military relations with traditional enemy Russia improved dramatically. Beginning in the mid-1990s, relations with Israel have been unusually close for an Islamic nation, based mainly on Israeli military and security assistance. However, after 2005 Israel's Palestine policy weakened support for this relationship among the Turkish public and in the Justice and Development Party (AKP) government. In the early 2000s, Turkey has cultivated closer relations with Syria, although the two countries have a long-standing dispute over distribution of water from the Euphrates River. Economic relations with Iran improved in the early 2000s, although Turkey consistently opposed Iran's development of nuclear weapons. Turkey has resisted Western pressure to end bilateral, energy-related programs with Iran, signing new electric power and natural gas agreements in mid-2008. Despite reservations about Kurdish autonomy in Iraq, Turkey has expressed readiness to establish relations with a new government in that country. In late 2007, tension rose with Iraq's government over Turkish incursions into the Kurdish provinces of Iraq in response to Kurdistan Workers' Party (PKK) activity in Turkey. Relations with Armenia have remained hostile because of Turkey's support for Azerbaijan in its unresolved Nagorno–Karabakh conflict with Armenia and ongoing disagreement about the Armenian deaths of 1915.

Membership in International Organizations: Among the international organizations of which Turkey is a member are the Asian Development Bank, Bank for International Settlements, Black Sea Economic Cooperation Pact, Council of Europe, Economic Cooperation Organization, Euro-Atlantic Partnership Council, European Bank for Reconstruction and Development, European Court of Human Rights, Food and Agriculture Organization, International Atomic Energy Agency, International Bank for Reconstruction and Development, International Civil Aviation Organization, International Criminal Police Organization (Interpol), International Development Association, International Federation of Red Cross and Red Crescent Societies, International Finance Corporation, International Fund for Agricultural Development, International Labour Organization, International Maritime Organization, International Monetary Fund, International Organization for Migration, International Telecommunication Union, Islamic Development Bank, North Atlantic Treaty Organization (NATO), Nuclear Energy Agency, Nuclear Suppliers Group, Organisation for the Prohibition of Chemical Weapons, Organization for Economic Co-operation and Development, Organization for Security and Co-operation in Europe, Organization of the Islamic Conference, Pollution Control Agency, United Nations, United Nations Committee on Trade and Development, United Nations Educational, Scientific and Cultural Organization, United Nations Industrial Development Organization, Universal Postal Union, World Customs Organization, World Federation of Trade Unions, World Health Organization, World Intellectual Property Organization, World Tourism Organization, and World Trade Organization. Turkey is an applicant for membership in the European Union.

Major International Treaties: Among the multilateral treaties to which Turkey is a signatory are the Basel Convention on the Control of Transboundary Movements of Hazardous Wastes and Their Disposal, Comprehensive Test Ban Treaty, Convention on Biological Diversity, Convention on the International Trade in Endangered Species of Wild Flora and Fauna, Convention on Long-Range Transboundary Air Pollution, conventions prohibiting the development, production, stockpiling, and use of biological and chemical weapons (known, respectively, as the Biological Weapons Convention and the Chemical Weapons Convention), Energy Charter Treaty, Geneva Conventions, Montreal Protocol on Substances that Deplete the Ozone Layer, Ramsar Convention on Wetlands, Treaty on the Non-Proliferation of Nuclear Weapons, United Nations Convention to Combat Desertification, and United Nations Framework Convention on Climate Change and its Kyoto Protocol.

NATIONAL SECURITY

Armed Forces Overview: Turkey's armed forces, the second largest in the North Atlantic Treaty Organization (NATO), are mainly made up of conscripts commanded by a cadre of professional soldiers. In 2008 the army had 402,000 active personnel, the navy had 48,600, and the air force had 60,100. Of the active personnel, about 360,000 in the army and navy were conscripts. In addition, some 379,000 were in the reserves and 150,000 in active and reserve components of the National Guard. Turkey contributes troops to several United Nations and NATO peacekeeping operations as well as maintaining a significant force in Turkish Cyprus. In 1998 a major expansion of the domestic arms industry began with the aim of withstanding an arms embargo such as the one imposed by the United States in the mid-1970s after the Cyprus conflict. In 2008 plans called for doubling the domestic contribution to total procurement, from 25 percent to 50 percent. The Ministry of Defense nominally controls the military, but in fact the chief of the General Staff, the most powerful figure in the military, enjoys substantial autonomy. Among the requirements for Turkey's membership in the European Union is that the military be brought fully under civilian control.

Foreign Military Relations: In 1996 Turkey signed two military cooperation agreements with Israel, making it the first Muslim state to establish such a relationship with that country. Between 1996 and 2002, military and economic ties between the two countries blossomed. The two shared training exercises and intelligence information and cooperated on joint security and weapons projects. However, in the early 2000s Turkey condemned Israeli actions against Palestine, cooling the relationship. In 2005 Israel and Turkey signed a new round of joint military production agreements. Turkey participated actively in the United States–led war on terrorism, maintaining 760 non-combat troops in Afghanistan as of 2008 and assuming the rotating command of the North Atlantic Treaty Organization (NATO)'s International Security Assistance Force in that country in 2002 and 2005. However, because of the Kurdish situation, Turkey blocked U.S. troop movement into Iraq at the onset of Operation Iraqi Freedom in 2003. In 2002 Turkey was granted an advisory role in military operations of the European Union (EU). In the early 2000s, nearly all of Turkey's arms acquisitions have been from EU countries or Israel; in 2007 it was the fourth-largest importer of arms in the world.

External Threat: Beginning in the 1960s, regional disputes have brought Turkey and Greece close to war on several occasions. Although general relations have improved, in the early 2000s negotiators failed to negotiate a treaty ending the Cyprus crisis, and Greece has continued to press its claim of 12 miles of territorial waters from the Greek islands of the Aegean Sea. In 2003 the U.S. invasion of Iraq increased Turkey's fears that Kurds from northern Iraq would unite with Kurds in southeastern Turkey to renew claims for an autonomous or independent Kurdistan. That issue remained in the background of relations with Iraq and the United States in 2008.

Defense Budget: The official defense expenditure for 2003 was US$8.1 billion and US$8.5 billion for 2004. The official figure for 2005 was US$8.1 billion, increasing to US$8.3 billion in 2006 and to US$10.9 billion in 2007. Official budget amounts do not include funding for the National Guard (which is under the Ministry of Interior) or for procurement from the Turkish defense industries. The 10-year program to upgrade the defense industry received an initial allocation of US$31 billion in 2005.

Major Military Units: In 2007 the army had 2 infantry divisions, 17 armored brigades, 15 mechanized infantry brigades, 11 infantry brigades, 5 commando brigades, 8 training brigades, 4 aviation regiments, 1 attack helicopter battalion, and 3 aviation battalions. The air force had 11 squadrons of ground attack fighters, 7 squadrons of fighter jets, 2 reconnaissance squadrons, 5 transport squadrons, 1 special forces command headquarters, and 4 surface-to-air missile squadrons. The naval forces were divided into the Northern Sea Area Command, the Southern Sea Area Command, and the Naval Training and Education Command. One regiment of marines (3,100 troops) also was on active duty. The air force had two tactical air forces and six surface-to-air missile squadrons.

Major Military Equipment: In 2007 the army had 4,205 main battle tanks, 250 armored reconnaissance vehicles, 650 armored infantry fighting vehicles, 830 armored personnel carriers, more than 685 pieces of towed artillery, 868 pieces of self-propelled artillery, 84 multiple rocket launchers, 5,813 mortars, 1,283 antitank guided weapons, 3,869 recoilless launchers, 1,664 antiaircraft guns, 935 surface-to-air missiles, 168 aircraft, 215 unmanned aerial vehicles, 37 attack helicopters, and 243 support helicopters. The navy had 13 submarines, 24 frigates, 24 missile combat vessels, 28 patrol craft, 1 minelayer, 23 mine countermeasures vessels, 8 amphibious vessels, 27 support vessels, and 16 armed helicopters. The air force had 480 combat aircraft, 40 support helicopters, no attack helicopters, and 178 surface-to-air missiles.

Military Service: The majority of military personnel are conscripted. At age 19, males are eligible to be conscripted for a 15-month tour of active duty, which was shortened from 18 months in 2003. University graduates may be conscripted as reserve officers for a 12-month period. The reserve obligation extends to age 41 for all services.

Paramilitary Forces: The National Guard, or Jandarma, includes 100,000 active personnel and a reserve of 50,000, under the command of the Ministry of Interior in peacetime and the Ministry of Defense in wartime. Included are one border division and three brigades, one of which is a commando brigade. Between 1988 and 2004, border security was the responsibility of the military; the Ministry of Interior reassumed this duty to meet a European Union requirement. The Coast Guard has 2,200 active-duty personnel, including 1,400 conscripts. Another 1,050 navy personnel are detailed to the Coast Guard.

Foreign Military Forces: Turkey hosts the headquarters of the North Atlantic Treaty Organization (NATO) Joint Command Southeast at İzmir. In 2005 that installation included some 1,650 U.S. Air Force personnel.

Military Forces Abroad: In 2007 Turkey had 36,000 troops, including two infantry divisions, in the Turkish Republic of Northern Cyprus. Turkey also had 760 troops with the International

Stabilization Force in Afghanistan, 253 with the stabilization force in Bosnia, 940 with the Kosovo Force in Serbia, and 746 with the United Nations Interim Force in Lebanon. Three Turkish observers served in the Temporary International Presence in Hebron (Palestine), and five were in Georgia. In 2005 Turkey took a second turn in command of the International Stabilization Force. Because of strong public disapproval of the war in Iraq, no Turkish troops participated in the United States–led Operation Iraqi Freedom.

Police: The National Police, under the Ministry of Interior, are responsible for security in urban areas. Under the central directorate of this force are sub-directorates for each province and district command posts for most administrative districts. Specialized units deal with problems such as narcotics and smuggling. The exact size of the police force is not known. The 100,000-member paramilitary National Guard, or Jandarma, also under the Ministry of Interior except for wartime situations, is responsible for security outside urban areas—about 90 percent of Turkey's territory. Jandarma officers come from the military academy, and recruits are conscripted. In the early 2000s, Turkey responded to international human rights pressure by revising the training of its Jandarma and National Police, which had a longstanding reputation for brutality and corruption. Younger police cadets now are sought to undergo a much longer training program emphasizing human rights. After being established in 1985 as an official force to supplement the military in Kurdish regions of southeastern Turkey, the paramilitary village guards became a semi-independent vigilante force in the 1990s, accused of a variety of criminal and human rights violations. In 2007 that force was estimated at 57,000. In 2004 parliament established a judicial police force, under the administration of the Ministry of Interior, to assist prosecutors in investigating criminal cases.

Internal Threat: Because of its location, Turkey is a major transfer point on east–west drug smuggling routes, particularly those moving heroin from southwestern Asia into Europe. Drug-related crimes such as money laundering also are common. However, the rate of violent crime and street crime is relatively low. The Kurdistan Workers' Party (PKK), the main Kurdish terrorist organization, officially renounced terror in 1999 but resumed attacks in 2004. PKK activity escalated steadily between 2004 and 2008, when Turkey attacked PKK strongholds in northern Iraq.

Terrorism: Beginning in 1984, Turkey suffered waves of terrorist activity by the Kurdistan Workers' Party (PKK). Urban terrorism increased sharply in the early 1990s. Many incidents were attributed to the radical Islamist group Dev Sol, which attacked Western targets in response to the Persian Gulf War of 1991. In the 1990s and early 2000s, Dev Sol and its successor organization, the Revolutionary People's Liberation Party, launched assassinations and other attacks against Turkish authorities and Westerners, but activity waned after 2003. For extended periods of time in the early 1990s, the PKK was able to control significant territory in the southeast. After PKK leader Abdullah Öcalan was captured in 1999, the group announced a formal end to its terrorist campaign against Turkey. Renunciation of that status in 2004 resulted in escalating attacks from 2004 through 2007. Although in 2007 Turkish Hezbollah (a separate group from the Lebanese Hezbollah) and the Great Eastern Islamic Raiders Front were considered the strongest Islamic terrorist organizations in Turkey, neither was believed capable of large-scale attacks. Flexibility in dealing with asymmetric warfare is a key element of the military reorganization plan for the early 2000s.

Human Rights: In the early 2000s, the position of Turkey's large Kurdish minority remained the largest ethnic human rights issue. Some improvement occurred in the Kurds' status after governments had blocked public assemblies and the distribution of literature by Kurdish groups. In 2002 the rights of Kurds were expanded, together with a broader human rights reform program. In 2003 Turkey passed extensive reforms to comply with the human rights standards of the European Union (EU). Reforms included imposing harsher sentences for enforcement personnel convicted of torture, improving the availability of lawyers to accused individuals, allowing media broadcasts in Kurdish and other minority languages, and making it possible for a civilian to head the National Security Council. The death penalty was abolished for civil crimes in peacetime. However, human rights groups reported that implementation of these reforms was slow. In 2007 arbitrary arrest and detention occurred, assembly and association were restricted occasionally, pretrial detention and judicial trials were overly long, the government still appeared to influence the outcome of some trials, and prisons remained overcrowded. Although the criminal code of 2005 redefined torture and ill treatment of prisoners and significantly increased sentences for those crimes, in 2007 accounts of malfeasance by security forces increased. The judicial police, established in 2004 to streamline prosecutorial investigations, reportedly have not been effective. The government has limited the activities of the media and harassed journalists expressing controversial views. In December 2005, the trial of novelist Orhan Pamuk for writings allegedly insulting the Turkish nation received international attention. (The next year, Pamuk won the Nobel Prize for Literature.) In 2008 the parliament narrowed the applicability of the law under which Pamuk was tried. In 2007 restriction of Internet communication began as courts blocked access to some Web sites.

The right to practice religion generally has been respected. However, the state has limited financial, training, and organizational activities of non-Muslim religious organizations; the EU has urged the reopening of the Greek Orthodox Halkı Seminary in Istanbul, which the government closed in 1985. Muslim activities have been circumscribed when undertaken in state-run institutions, and the state Directorate of Religious Affairs, responsible to the prime minister, oversees the operation of all religious institutions. Violence against women, particularly spousal abuse, is very common, and few victims file complaints. Honor killings of "disgraced" female family members continue in rural areas. Turkey is a destination and a transit point for a moderate amount of trafficking in women and children, with complicity by corrupt police. Human rights organizations have demanded that Turkey draw up a new constitution because of human rights violations inherent in the present document, which was written in 1982 under a military regime.